I Am a Tree

This book is dedicated to all the people in my life who have helped me to grow.

Stand up tall and be a tree

I am a tree
I am a tree
If you were a tree
Which tree would you be?

I am an Oak tree, wide, tall and proud
My roots go deep into the ground
From an acorn I have grown
Birds come to me to make their homes

Can you stand up tall and proud?
Just like the tree plant your feet in the ground,
Lift your arms up
Tall and wide
Puff out you cheeks
Show all your pride.

I am a Beech tree,
Like a silver fountain
I shoot into the air
My leaves sound like metal
As the wind blows through them

I sound like the sea,
People love to sit by me

Can you stand up tall
Like a fountain?
Sparkling into the sky
Tall as a mountain.

I am a tree I am a tree
If I were a tree
Which tree would I be?

I am a big Horse Chestnut tree
Everyone knows me as
The conker tree
I make conkers in spiky cases
Children's delight
Through the ages

Can you stand up tall like me?
Pretend to be a conker tree.

I am an Ash tree,
Part of the Olive family
I stand gracefully with my family
Children draw me for I look around
Did you know my seeds have wings
- they fly and twirl down to the ground.

Can you twirl and spin like my seeds?

I am a tree I am a tree
If I were a tree
Which tree would I be?

I am a weeping Willow tree
I came from a country called China for all to see me
My branches fall right down to the ground
If you sit under me
I have healing properties
You can hide in my green tent
For a while.

I am called a Silver Birch tree
I belong to a larger family
-called Betulaceae (bet-oo-la-see)- that is
Latin to you and me!
I have a white peeling paper-like trunk
Which has some medicinal properties.

I am also a deciduous tree,
Which means my triangle like leaves
Turn yellow and brown,
And in the Autumn, fall to the ground

Can you be like the leaf
That lets go of the branch
To gently twirl down to the ground?

I am a tree I am a tree
If I were a tree
Which tree would I be?

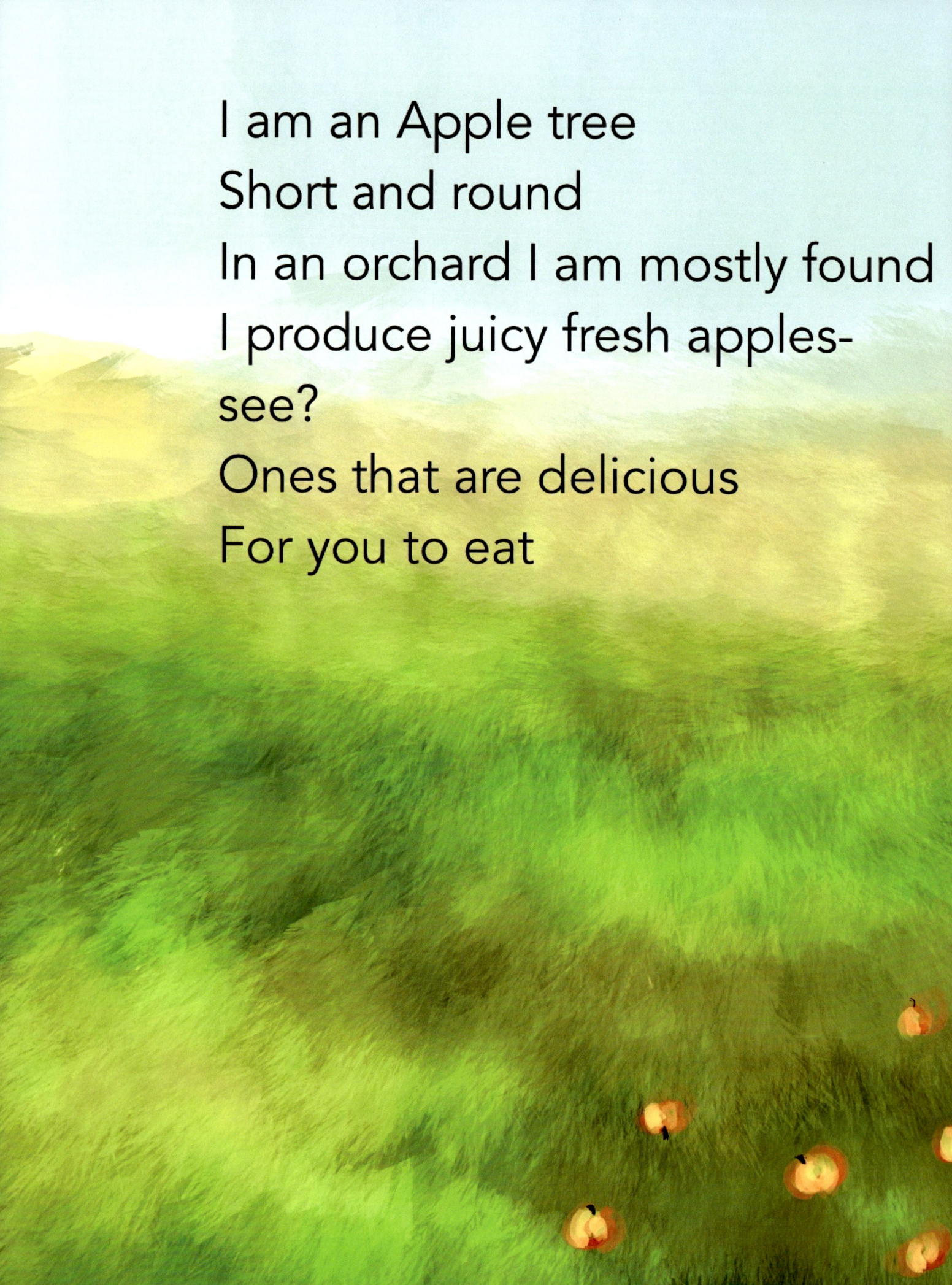

I am an Apple tree
Short and round
In an orchard I am mostly found
I produce juicy fresh apples-
see?
Ones that are delicious
For you to eat

Look around now
See now that
Some are tall
All have roots

Turn the page now

what can you see?
we are all trees.
some are round
into the ground

to see all the trees…

All together we dance
We are all different
But we

in the breeze ....are all TREES!!!!!

sounds in the wind.

🍁 Tree ID Nature Walk
Objective: Connect the trees from the book to real life.
Materials: Printable tree checklist or sketchbooks.
Activity:

1. Take a walk in a park or schoolyard.
2. Look for real-life versions of trees in the book.
3. Kids check off or draw what they find and share one fact they remember.

✂ Leaf Print Art

Objective: Combine creativity with sensory play.
Materials: Real leaves, paint, paper, sponges or rollers.
Activity:

1. Collect leaves (bonus points for matching book (trees.)
2. Paint one side and press onto paper.
3. Label the leaf and talk about it's trees special features.

🎵 "Tree Pose" Yoga Time

Objective: Promote balance, mindfulness and physical activity.
How to Play:

1. Teach kids simple "tree pose" from yoga.
2. Use calm music or nature sounds.

(Please turn page……)

3. While in pose, ask: "What kind of tree are you today?

🧠 **Tree Trivia Time**

Objective: reinforce facts from the book.
How to Play:
1. Ask questions like "Which tree has the longest roots? or "Which one bends instead of breaking?"
2. Turn it into a quiz with points or team play.

 **Draw Your Own Tree Page**

Objective: Inspire storytelling and creativity.
Activity:

1. Give kids a blank double-page spread template.
2. Ask them to invent a new tree character and write a short rhyme about it.
3. Display their creations as a classroom art gallery.

Here are two blank pages where you can draw your own beautiful trees:

Blessed is the person who walks

    not in the counsel of the wicked,

    nor stands in the way of sinners,

    nor sits in the seat of scoffers;

    Such are like a tree

    planted by streams of water

    that yields fruit in its season,

  and its leaf does not wither,

    In all that these do, they prosper.

                              Psalm 1:3

Other books by this Author and Illustrator -

The Butterfly Who Wouldn't Open Her Wings

The Plum Tree

Fox & Dog

Phil the Brill Krill

Flesh

Haelan

About the Author

　　Isabel Bee is an MFA (Middlesex University UK), RA shortlisted artist, poet, violin player and chronic illness warrior. She lives in the UK with her family and a dog. Isabel illustrates all her own books. All books are available from Waterstones, Goodreads and good bookstores and Amazon.

www.ingramcontent.com/pod-product-compliance
Lightning Source LLC
Chambersburg PA
CBRC090840010526
44119CB00045B/499